Angels

AMONG US

Angels

AMONG US

INCREDIBLE PHOTOGRAPHS
OF ANGELS IN EVERYDAY LIFE

SKYE ALEXANDER

D&C
David and Charles

A DAVID & CHARLES BOOK
© F&W Media International, LTD 2011

David & Charles is an imprint of F&W Media International, LTD
Brunel House, Forde Close, Newton Abbot, TQ12 4PU, UK

F&W Media International, LTD is a subsidiary of F+W Media Inc.
4700 East Galbraith Road, Cincinnati, OH 45236, USA

First published in the UK and USA in 2011

Text © Skye Alexander 2011

A catalogue record for this book is available from the
British Library.

ISBN-13: 978-0-7153-3851-3 hardback
ISBN-10: 0-7153-3851-X hardback

Printed in China by RR Donnelley
for F&W Media International, LTD
Brunel House, Forde Close, Newton Abbot, TQ12 4PU, UK

Acquisitions Editor Neil Baber
Editor Sarah Callard
Project Editor Cathy Joseph
Senior Designer Jodie Lystor
Senior Production Controller Kelly Smith

F+W Media Inc. publishes high-quality books on a wide
range of subjects. For more great book ideas visit:
www.rubooks.co.uk

Contents

Introduction

We seem to have an innate need to believe in benevolent beings and a mystical realm beyond what we experience in our everyday lives here on earth. For thousands of years, people around the globe, from myriad cultures and belief systems, have sought and received assistance from heavenly helpers. Today, when so much of our world seems baffling, overwhelming, or totally out of control, perhaps it's no coincidence that angels seem to be showing up in large numbers to guide us on life's perilous journey.

In 2008, *The Washington Post* conducted a poll of 36,000 adults in the US from various religious and non-religious backgrounds. It found that most Americans think angels actively participate in our lives, and more than 80 per cent believe miracles occur.

Many people say they experience the presence of angels during life-threatening situations or periods of hopelessness and despair. Russian artist Marc Chagall, for example, was shaken by self-doubt and ready to give up his profession when one bleak night a rustling of wings woke him from a sound sleep. A brilliant blue light illuminated his bedroom and a beautiful winged creature hovered above him. Chagall believed the angel had appeared to inspire and encourage him. For the rest of his life he continued to paint angels, which he considered manifestations of the highest form of love.

'Most Americans think angels actively participate in our lives ...'

Angels frequently help us resolve earthly conundrums. Some of the world's greatest geniuses, including Leonardo da Vinci and Albert Einstein, admitted receiving insight and guidance from higher sources. Often these insights come to us in the form of epiphanies – 'ah-ha' moments – as if the sun suddenly emerged from behind a cloud and chased away the shadows in our minds. Other times awarenesses present themselves in dreams, meaningful events and 'coincidences', or through people who seem to have been sent to us at just the right moment, precisely for that purpose. Medical personnel and hospice workers often witness beings of light nearby when someone dies. It's as if celestial tour guides show up, ready to shepherd the newly released soul into the wondrous world on the other side. People who have undergone near-death experiences regularly recount tales of being warmly greeted by luminous entities who resonate with love, peace and joy.

After Jay Bailey of Kerrville, Texas was critically injured in a motor accident, he found himself in a place permeated by radiant light. He recognized his mother and father standing nearby, as well as a powerful being dressed in a translucent ivory-coloured suit that glowed, whom he refers to as the Brilliant One. Bailey felt safe, secure and completely accepted. As he describes it, 'The atmosphere is love; we feel such joy in togetherness.' The Brilliant One gave Bailey a choice: to stay in this blissful realm or return to earth. When he chose to return, he says, 'I saw the Brilliant One pick me up and proceed into my body, head first. Liquid life-fluid flowed into my body.' He awoke in the hospital after lying comatose for two weeks.

In his book *The Evolution Angel*, Todd Michael OD, an emergency and trauma physician who witnessed more than 500 deaths, explains there really aren't any angels, per se. What we interpret as angels are emanations of an omnipresent, loving, divine energy that pervades our universe. 'The "angels," the "messengers," are just [God's] way of showing himself in such a way that we can actually handle it.'

In this book, you'll read stories from people of all ages, nationalities, and walks of life who reveal their encounters with angels. Many of them believe that during their darkest hours, angels visited them to provide protection, bring messages of hope, or offer miraculous healing. Some of their experiences are very personal; others are shared by large numbers of people. But these stories are more than mere recollections – they are accompanied by photos of the angels themselves.

What do Angels Look Like?

If asked this question, most people would probably describe angels as looking pretty much like beautiful humans, but with large feathered wings and halos. For the most part, however, the photos in this book show patterns of radiant white or brilliantly coloured light. Some of the shapes resemble human forms, although they tend to be translucent and fuzzy, such as the angel supposedly photographed from an aeroplane window. Some, like the angel in the fountain at the Dollywood Theme Park in Tennessee, USA, seem to sport wing-like appendages. Many appear simply as nebulous orbs, rays, splashes, or streaks of light.

Hebrew religious texts and the Bible discuss angels, but not until the Book of Revelations does the author, St John, describe in much detail what the angels looked like. According to Muslim belief, an angel with 140 pairs of wings brought the Qur'an to Mohammed. Ancient Greek mythology portrays Hermes, the messenger of the gods, with wings either on his feet or his helmet. Norse tradition says the Valkyries – heavenly female warriors – rode winged horses into battlefields and ferried the bravest men from among the slain to a celestial realm called Valhalla. As they crossed the rainbow bridge between earth and heaven, they created the brilliant Northern Lights.

Our conceptions of angels mostly come from the renderings of artists over the centuries. It's interesting to trace the evolution of angels in art to see how earthly ideas influenced depictions of the divine realm. The earliest known image of a winged angel is featured in a mosaic in a Roman

church and dates back to the 5th century. After that, artists regularly portrayed angels with wings.

During the Middle Ages, artists used images to convey biblical stories to the illiterate masses. Beautiful, if solemn, angels were shown taking charge of earthly matters, rather than lounging on heavenly thrones. Renaissance artists, including Michelangelo, Leonardo da Vinci, Raphael, Botticelli, Rembrandt and Dürer, gave us images of powerful, avenging angels who combated the forces of evil. The archangel Michael, especially, was often painted wielding a mighty sword against demons and dragons. In the opulent Rococo period, artists transformed angels into lush, sensual, sentimental creatures. A century later, the Victorians nudged out the romantic angels in favour of more serious and virginal guardians.

'The earliest known image of a winged angel dates back to the 5th century.'

According to some contemporary angel researchers, angels abide among us all the time. Only rarely, and often under extreme circumstances, do they make themselves visible to us. They can assume any form they choose, not just the winged-and-haloed version that fits our preconceptions. Unlike humans, who are confined in physical bodies and change appearance gradually, over an extended period of time, angels are composed of an exquisitely fine material similar to light, which allows them to shift and change constantly, much like a flickering flame. That may explain why most of the photos in this book show luminous, amorphous shapes, rather than beings that resemble the sculptures and paintings that adorn Europe's great cathedrals and museums.

Different Types of Angels

Like our modern corporations, the heavenly realm is organized into tiers of angels at different levels who perform specific duties. At least that's how the Christian mystic Dionysius the Areopagite described it 1500 years ago in his study, The Celestial Hierarchy. In the 13th century, the Dominican priest and philosopher St Thomas Aquinas expanded upon Dionysius's work in his Summa Theologica.

Both scholars postulated nine types of angels, ordered into ranks according to their actions and responsibilities.

• Our guardian angels occupy the lowest level, closest to earth. These divine beings watch over humans, guiding and protecting us, conveying messages from the heavens and assisting us in times of need. When we experience angelic interventions, communications and other forms of assistance, we're interacting with this type of angel.

• The archangels exist on the rung just above angels, where they assist the forces of nature.

• Above them are the principalities (or princes), who guard and guide individual nations. According to Judeo-Christian scriptures, each nation/culture has its own heavenly representative.

• Next come the powers, which fight evil and safeguard the universe.

• The virtues, the miracle workers of the cosmos, reside on the next level.

• Above them, the dominions serve as heavenly managers who direct the other angels.

• On the next tier, the thrones (also known as

orphanim) act as judges who mete out justice
in both the heavenly and earthly realms.

• Next in line are the cherubim, who maintain the stars
in the heavens and keep the 'Akashic Records,' which
supposedly chronicle all the knowledge in the universe.

• The seraphim occupy the highest rung of the celestial
ladder, closest to God. Their singing is said to aid the process
of creation.

Can Everybody see Angels?

Angels, it seems, can and do appear to all sorts of people – even
nonbelievers. In fact, they may be present in our lives all the
time, holding our hands, watching our backs, and whispering
in our ears. If F. Forrester Church, author of *Entertaining Angels*,
is right, 'Every moment of every day is riddled by their traces.'

Many of the people who contributed to this book already
believed in angels before they took these astonishing
photographs. Actually seeing angels, however, strengthened
their faith – and in some cases changed their lives forever.

When angels communicate with sceptics, they often
choose a more commonplace method, such as dreams
to get their point across. 'It is not that sceptics do not
experience the mysterious and divine,' bestselling author
Sophy Burnham explains in *A Book of Angels*, 'but rather
that the mysteries are presented to them in such a flat and
factual, everyday, reasonable way so as not to disturb.'

*'Actually seeing angels
strengthened their faith ...'*

Thousands of people around the world have photographed
what they think are angels – the website www.angelsghosts.
com is a great place to see lots of amazing and thought-
provoking pictures. Countless others say they've experienced
angelic contacts of some kind. You, too, may have encountered
an angel, you just didn't realize it at the time. Perhaps an
angel is hovering right beside you at this very moment.

Anomalies in Angel Photographs

Darkroom tricks, airbrushing, double exposures, and other smoke-and-mirror deceptions have long existed in the world of photography. Digital cameras and sophisticated computer technology, however, have made altering photographs easier than ever. E. Joe Deering, veteran photojournalist for the *Houston Chronicle*, explains that doctored images often show slight variations in pixels (points in a graphic image), which can be detected when the picture is enlarged. Differences in lighting may also reveal a fraudulent photo.

Intentional manipulation aside, many photographs feature unexpected and unexplained images of things that the photographer knows weren't there when he looked through the lens and pressed the shutter. When careful analysis fails to clarify the conundrum, the peculiarity is known as an anomaly. Merriam Webster's *Collegiate Dictionary* defines the term anomaly as an

'irregularity…something different, abnormal, peculiar, or not easily classified.' A genuine photographic anomaly is something not caused by dust, particles, scratches, or damage to the film. Nor have mishaps occurred during developing or handling the film. The inexplicable image is sealed into the silver halide of the film, just like the other recognizable images, as happened when photo technician James Patryck Jordan developed the photograph of two girls praying.

But its mysterious quality doesn't necessarily mean the anomaly lies outside the natural realm — only that we don't understand what it is or how it came to be part of the photo. Many common anomalies are created by the camera, lighting, or environment. Usually, the photographer isn't aware of the situation that is responsible for causing the anomaly. Therefore, when viewing the photo, he may believe an eerie light or odd shadowy shape depicts something otherworldly. Undoubtedly, some of the photographs presented in this book fall into this category.

Common Photographic Anomalies and Their Causes

Orbs are among the most frequently seen anomalies. These spheres of light may be produced by light reflecting off a shiny surface such as a window, mirror, or the polished metal of a nearby automobile. Lens flare (when the sun's light shines on the camera lens) generates strange light effects, too. Dust or pollen in the air can also cause orbs to show up on film, as can moisture from water vapour, mist, rain, or snow – even if the atmospheric condition is so slight the photographer doesn't notice it at the time she snaps the picture. Even insects flying by may cause orbs to appear in photos.

Wispy, cloudy, or foggy images turn up with regularity in photographs as well. Usually, however, the camera has not captured the ectoplasm of a spirit, although the image may be shaped like an angel or ghostly figure. In some instances, fog, steam, or rain probably caused the peculiarity. Smoke from a cigarette or fire also can produce this result. In cold weather, someone's breath could generate this type of anomaly.

Streaks of light might seem to be brilliant rays emanating from a heavenly being or from a physical person's supercharged etheric energy field. However, a camera's flash can generate these streaks, especially when the photographer takes a picture at night using an extended exposure and moves the camera. Ambient light or light bouncing off reflective surfaces may also result in bright streaks.

Translucent or shadowy figures, though less common than other anomalies, sometimes show up unexpectedly in photographs. But what looks like an angel may actually be the image of a person reflected in a window or mirror. Extended exposure settings can also cause ghostly outlines – particularly if someone moves – as can the slight flash delays on some digital cameras. Orange hazy glows and light bars may also be produced in this way.

Does the Photo Show a Real Angel?

You've captured an eerie image on camera – and you're absolutely certain no one has intentionally tampered with the photo. Is what you see really an angel or other spirit being? Dr Melvyn Willin, honorary archivist for The Society for Psychical Research in London and author of *Ghosts Caught on Film*, recommends asking yourself the following questions:

• Was the film flawed in any way?

• Did an accident occur while processing the film?

• Did the photographer simply not notice the presence of the unexplained image at the time she took the picture?

• Could the strange image have been caused by a light effect, such as lens flare or a reflection?

• If the anomaly is genuine, could the image have been produced by a natural effect, even if you don't understand that effect?

• Does the photo actually show something paranormal?

• Does the appearance of this unusual image strengthen your belief in angels and otherworldly entities?

• Have you considered all the possibilities?

Most of the people who took the photographs presented in this book have no intention of creating a deception – except the protagonists in the Doidge Angel Caper. Yet some of the anomalies can be explained by natural causes, even if we don't know exactly what those causes might be. Genuinely baffling photos do turn up, however, and may truly depict nonphysical entities. The most intriguing apparitions are those witnessed and photographed by numerous people. The 'Lady of Light,' who regularly appeared above St Mary's Coptic Church in Zeitoun, Egypt over a period of more than two years, is a good example.

One person's plume of smoke is another person's angel. In the end, the important question may not be is this the picture of a real angel? What matters is the impact the picture has on those who view it. Many of the people whose photos and stories appear in this book received comfort, hope, guidance, inspiration and healing from what they believe to be angels. Some have treasured their angel pictures for decades and say the photos strengthened their faith in a divine presence.

As the Rev. John Westerhoff, a pastoral theologian at Duke University's Divinity School, explained in a *Time* magazine article, 'Angels exist through the eyes of faith, and faith is perception. Only if you can perceive it can you experience it.'

Snowflake Orbs

Snowflakes and raindrops frequently cause glowing orbs to appear in photographs. Light from the camera's flash – especially in a picture taken at night, as this one was – makes the snowflakes sparkle and seem almost otherworldly. In this case, the photographer knew the snowflakes produced the orbs, not angels.

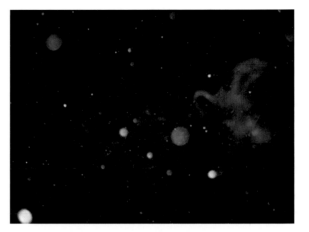

Wanda Walks with an Angel

It had just started snowing on Christmas Eve, 2004, when Susana took this photo of her mother, Wanda, walking with an angel. In their hometown of Pasadena, Texas, USA (about ten miles outside of Houston), snow is a rare occurrence.

This picture shows a good example of mist or fog, which the photographer doesn't notice at the time, being captured on film and mistaken as something paranormal. Most likely, moisture in the air on a winter night caused the cloudy image that appears to the right of Wanda – although perhaps it really is an angel joining the women on the holiday evening.

Parking Lot Angel

Katie Hoag from Renton, Washington, USA took this photo in 2005 in front of a movie theatre. Although it appears to show ectoplasm, a substance from which spirits are supposedly composed, more likely the odd glow was caused by lighting from the movie marquee. Or, the camera's flash might have reflected off the nearby vehicles in the parking lot. Often, the photographer doesn't notice this at the time she snaps the shutter, and believes she's captured a spirit on film.

Streaks of Coloured Light

Although Shawnda from Columbus, Ohio, USA says she'd like to believe angels attended
her brother's college graduation ceremony in 2005, she realizes the strange effects
shown here might have been due to her digital camera. This picture features the orange
glow and strange streaks of coloured light that can result when the photographer
uses an extended shutter speed indoors. Most likely, Shawnda moved the camera
while snapping this photo – although angels may have been present, too.

Early Spirit Photos

An offshoot of the Spiritualist Movement in the US, spirit photography, or 'spiritography', supposedly captures on film the spirits of deceased individuals. The belief that spirits live in our midst was popular and widespread during the late 19th and early 20th centuries. People who had lost loved ones consulted with mediums who claimed to communicate with the departed friends and relatives on the Other Side. In an attempt to prove that spirit beings were indeed present during a séance or other event, photographers ostensibly snapped pictures of the spirits. Frequently such photos showed a shadowy figure standing behind the person being photographed – although no one in the room at the time noticed the presence of the eerie figure.

The most notable of these early photographers was William H. Mumler, a Boston jewellery engraver who began experimenting with photography in the early 1860s and expanded his spiritography into a lucrative business after the American Civil War. His famous picture of Mary Todd Lincoln with the spirit of the deceased President standing behind her appears in this chapter. However, he was accused of fraud and brought to trial, where circus owner PT Barnum testified against him. Mumler allowed sceptics and experts to examine his photographs, cameras and complete developing process; nobody could determine how he achieved his results. Even though he was cleared of fraud charges, the trial ruined Mumler's career.

Many mediums and spiritographers turned out to be charlatans who employed an array of parlour tricks to part their customers from their money. Because séances usually took place in dimly lit rooms, photographers used long exposure settings. Subjects had to remain very still for a period of time in order to get a clear picture. If someone moved about or only remained within camera range for a few moments, a ghostly blur occurred. General ignorance of what was then a new technology allowed spiritographers to pull off this particular hoax, using human assistants to pose as 'spirits.' Other photographers superimposed images or used double exposures to create 'paranormal' results.

In another type of psychic photography, mediums such as Uri Geller mentally burned images onto photographic film. Instead of taking a picture directly of a spirit, the psychic serves as a channel for generating the photo by receiving images from the spirit world and then projecting them onto the film. Credible paranormal investigators, including Hans Holzer, have utilized this method.

Some of the intriguing pictures in this section show examples of common photography scams from the Victorian era. Others may actually record the presence of angels, ghosts, and other spirits among us.

Abraham Lincoln's Spirit Comforts his Widow

This famous photo was taken in New York City by William H. Mumler after the assassination of President Lincoln. In it, a transparent Lincoln appears to stand behind his widow, Mary Todd Lincoln, with his hands on her shoulders. According to some sources, Mumler didn't know the identity of his black-garbed subject until after he developed the photographs, believing her to be a woman named Mrs Tundall.

During the 1860s and '70s, Mumler became celebrated on both sides of the Atlantic as a photographer of the spirits of the dead. His book, *Personal Experiences of William H. Mumler in Spirit Photography*, discussed his methods and the subjects he photographed. Although he was accused of fraud and his work scrutinized by numerous experts at the time, he was never found guilty.

Did Mumler really capture the deceased President's spirit on film, during a moment of giving comfort to his widow? Or did the notorious photographer engage in a hoax too technically sophisticated for 19th century sceptics to detect?

'Although he was accused of fraud, Mumler was never found guilty ...'

An Angel Hovers Above a Farm During a Storm

According to the handwritten inscription, Sinklier and Blevins apparently snapped this striking photo of an angel during a storm in Wells, Kansas, USA In 1916. The lighter image in the sky looks like a huge, brilliant angel hovering in the ominous clouds above a farm. Sandy Wasmer explains the picture was discovered in her grandfather's family bible after his death. The words '1916 Arthur Hutchens – 4 Wells Kansas' are written on the back of the print. Wasmer, however, admits she's been unable to obtain further information about it from the Kansas Historical Society.

Is this simply a picture of the sun peeking through the clouds? Or did a guardian angel appear to protect this farm and its inhabitants during a potentially devastating storm?

'The lighter image in the sky looks like a huge, brilliant angel …'

Portraits of Deceased Loved Ones' Spirits?

These portraits supposedly show the presence of loved ones' spirits hovering near living relatives or friends. Photos such as these were intended to provide solace to those left behind on earth, and may have strengthened the subjects' faith in an afterlife. During the Victorian era, most people believed the spirit lived on after death. Unscrupulous mediums and other charlatans capitalized on that belief and used photos to 'prove' that the dead still cared about their grieving families and friends. However, it's likely early photographers doctored these spirit photos using double exposures or other tricks to produce the translucent images.

'These photos were intended to provide solace to those left behind on earth ...'

Guardian Angels

Guardian angels are the most familiar of all celestial beings. A poll conducted by Baylor University Institute for Studies of Religion in 2008 revealed a majority of Americans feel they have a personal angel looking after them. When 1,700 people were questioned, 55 per cent of the respondents stated they believed they had been 'protected from harm by a guardian angel.'

The Qur'an tells us that 'For every soul, there is a guardian watching it.' Both the Old and New Testaments of the Bible regularly mention guardian angels. In Matthew, for instance, St Jerome explains: 'Each one has from his birth an angel commissioned to guard it.' The Talmud speaks of guardian angels being assigned both to individuals and to nations. The ancient Assyrians and Babylonians also believed in these benevolent beings – a figure of a guardian angel that once adorned an Assyrian palace is now in the British Museum. The early Greeks thought each person had a daemon who guided him throughout his life; the Romans called a man's guardian a genius and a woman's a juno. The native people of North and South America often connect with their spirit guides during vision quests and may depict their tribe's spirit guardians in totem poles and other artwork.

According to some belief systems, animals and plants have spirit guardians called devas who aid their growth and evolution. Deva is a Sanskrit word that means 'shining one.' Peter and Eileen Caddy and Dorothy Maclean, who founded the Findhorn Community in northeast Scotland, collaborated with the devas in order to produce amazingly abundant gardens under extremely unfavourable conditions.

Most of the time, our guardian angels remain invisible to us as they perform their duties. Sometimes they appear in seemingly human form as 'good Samaritans' who assist us in times of need. And occasionally, we may even capture them on film, as many of the people in this section believe they've done.

An Angel Responds to Girls' Prayers

James Patryck Jordan's evening at a Walmart Fuji photo lab began like any other. Working alone as he often did, the photo technician carefully prized open the sealed housing of a Fujifilm Quicksnap Flash 400 35mm disposable camera that had just been dropped off for processing and sent the film to the developing machine. Fifteen minutes later, a strip of negatives emerged from the developer. Jordan fed the strip into the lab's printer computer and viewed the enlarged images on the computer screen. The last frame, he said, 'immediately caught my attention.' The photo showed two female figures with bowed heads. But an inexplicable image appeared above them: a strange, brilliant red-orange orb of light, and within the orb a pale, illuminated figure. With gloved hands, Jordan removed the negative strip and examined it closely. 'There were no particles or scratches on the negative. This was not dust.' The image was sealed into the silver halide of the film. He couldn't explain the anomaly.

When the owner returned an hour later to pick up the photos, Jordan showed her the curious image and asked her about it. The woman started crying. She told Jordan she'd been camping with her daughters when they heard a radio report of an escaped convict in the area. The two sisters knelt beside the campfire and prayed for protection. Was the anomaly Jordan discovered simply the reflected glow of the fire? Or an angelic response to the girls' prayers? Jordan asked the woman if he could keep a copy of the photo and she agreed. 'For two years I saw 5000 frames per day, five days a week,' he said. 'Never did anything like this ever show up, before or after.'

'The two sisters knelt beside the campfire and prayed for protection …'

Angel Seen from an Aeroplane Window?

In 1972, Elaine Fontes was at work in a photo lab in Fort Lauderdale, Florida, when the printer called the entire staff over to see something incredible. She'd just developed a roll of film a customer had shot from the window of an aeroplane during a storm. One photo clearly showed a white-robed figure with outstretched arms, stepping out of the clouds. No one, including the printer, could explain the strange image. Some described it as an angel, perhaps guarding the plane; others saw it as Christ hovering in the sky. Fontes recalls the printer made a copy of the amazing photo for everyone who wanted one and claims, 'This is a legitimate picture – I saw the original with my own eyes!'

When the photo appeared on the website www.angelsghosts.com in 2005, it triggered a flurry of interest. Numerous other people, it seemed, also owned copies of the photo, including Kevin Schemenauer of Quesnel, British Columbia, whose aunt had given it to him in the early 1980s. Rick, from Tampa, Florida, remembers getting chills when a friend showed him the photo in 1977: 'He told me that his mother's friend had taken it from an airplane window during a storm.'

As more people came forward with copies of the remarkable photograph, different stories about its origins emerged. Elaine Douthat from Pearly Gates Ministries believes the photo was taken on the ground by an elderly woman in Spiro, Oklahoma who gave copies to 'nearly everybody in our church around 1976.' We may never know who really photographed this unexplained apparition, or where. Over the years, however, the picture has touched the lives of countless people and left a profound impression on many of them.

'Some described it as an angel, perhaps guarding the plane; others saw it as Christ hovering in the sky ...'

A Guardian Angel Protects Firefighters

In the late summer of 2006, Tami Jean Smith and her husband helped fight the Tripod Complex Fire that raged through Washington State, consuming nearly 70,000 acres. Tami Jean worked as a parts runner, while her husband drove a huge D8 Caterpillar dozer on the burning ridge.

'At the time she took the picture, the plane was the only thing in the sky ...'

As a fire bomber plane flew overhead, dropping retardant on the blaze, Tami Jean snapped this photograph. 'When I downloaded the photos I saw the illuminating light in the bottom right-hand corner,' she explains. But at the time she took the picture, 'the plane was the only thing in the sky.' She shot four more photos of the plane, but none of them showed the angel-shaped light in the sky. Is it a guardian angel protecting the firefighters as they performed their dangerous job?

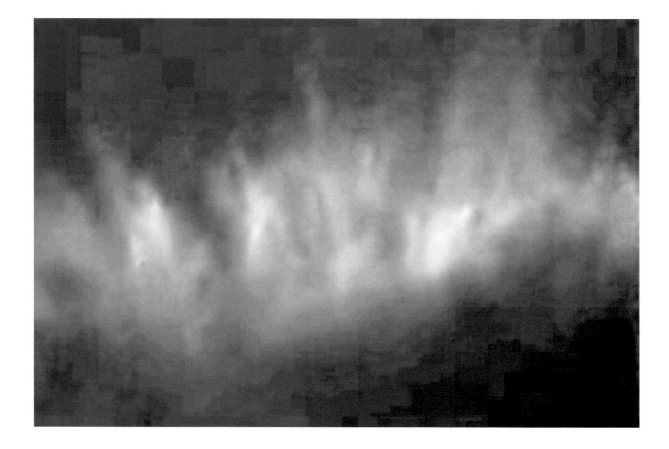

Guardian Angels Appear at an Earthquake

Ten minutes before a devastating earthquake shook Sichuan, China in 2008, spectacular and unexplained lights appeared in the sky. A video of the lights (from which this photo is extracted) shows brilliant colours, much like those in the Northern Lights or aurora borealis. Many people who saw the multicoloured light display believed they were witnessing the appearance of angels who had come to provide protection during the quake.

'Many who saw the light display believed they were witnessing the appearance of angels …'

Sceptics might claim seismic activity was responsible for the unusual lights, which Canadian neuro-psychologist Michael Persinger of Laurentian University has described as 'exotic luminous phenomena.' According to Norse mythology, however, the Northern Lights occur when angelic beings carry souls from earth to the heavens. Is this what happened during the Sichuan earthquake?

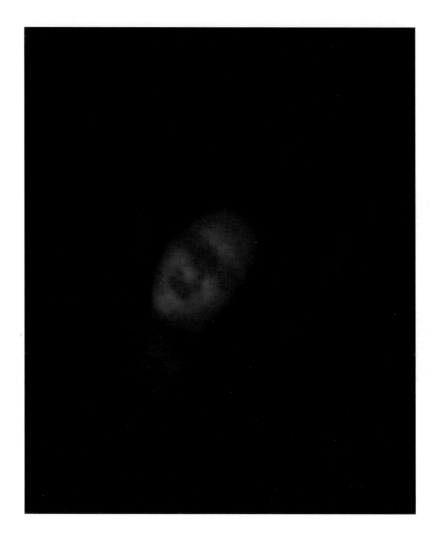

Family Guardian Angel Joins a Holiday Party

John Hazelbaker and his family celebrated US Independence Day 2007 with a party in Brazil, Indiana. Using his Nikon CoolPix 775 digital camera, Hazelbaker busily snapped photographs of aunts, uncles, sons, daughters, brothers and sisters. He also shot random pictures of the fireworks display overhead.

Later, when he downloaded the photos of the party, he spotted a 'relative' he hadn't realized was with them that night. In fact, Hazelbaker says, 'No one saw her in the sky.' Only his camera recorded her appearance.

It might be tempting to discount this image as an anomaly caused by illumination from the fireworks – or even a strange pattern of clouds on the moon. But the serene woman's face seems too perfect to be accidental. Hazelbaker's explanation? 'I do believe it is our angel.'

'The serene woman's face seems too perfect to be accidental …'

Hot Tub Angel

According to some angel researchers, angels are attracted to joyful, uplifting environments and situations – these light-hearted beings like to have fun. Maybe that's why this particular angel showed up to join Bobbi Myers and her sisters in November 1996 as they vacationed at a mountain retreat. At the time the photo was taken, none of the sisters realized the spirit was there with them as they soaked in the hot tub.

Myers has always believed her family has a guardian angel watching over them. In fact, many wisdom traditions teach that angels are assigned to guide and protect families, tribes, and even countries. But until she saw this photograph, Myers didn't have 'proof.'

Of course, it's easy to explain away this apparition as steam rising from the hot tub. But although steam does gather above the water in a hot tub, it doesn't usually accumulate in one place, as is the case here. Nor does it collect into such a human-shaped form. Furthermore, the misty image appears to be sitting outside the hot tub, not floating above it as would be expected if it were created by steam – and Myers attests that the tub didn't have outside vents that would allow steam to escape that way. Three different photography experts studied the picture and could arrive at no explanation for the anomaly. Perhaps it's just what Myers believes: their guardian angel enjoying a happy occasion with the family.

'None of the sisters realized the spirit was there with them as they soaked in the hot tub ...'

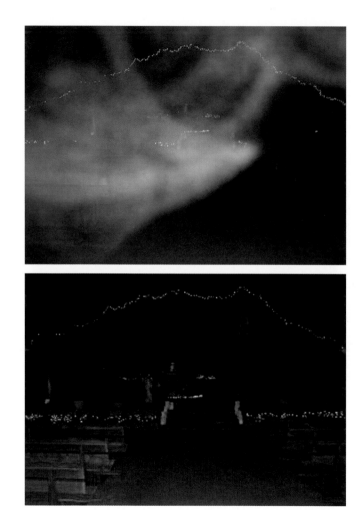

Crèche Angel

About 9pm on Christmas Eve, Gary stood before an outdoor crèche in Litchfield, Connecticut, USA. As he snapped pictures of the nativity scene with his digital camera on that cold, New England night, he suddenly felt a rush of warm air and saw a flash of light. He thought maybe his camera battery had exploded, and took a few more pictures to see if the camera had, indeed, broken. However, everything seemed to be in good working order.

When he got home and downloaded his photos, he saw something amazing. The picture of the surprising, luminous shape that seemed to soar in front of the crèche had been taken just as Gary felt the inexplicable warmth sweep through the chilly night. No one else was around at the time, no cars and no streetlights. As Gary explains, the crèche had been erected 'in an outdoor grotto, and it was a moonless night … very clear and crisp.' His photos show the scene as it appeared when he first arrived and again with the angel-like presence flying between him and the nativity. Although anomalies such as this can sometimes be caused by the photographer's breath in cold temperatures, the image seems too large to be explained this way.

'he suddenly felt a rush of warm air and saw a flash of light …'

The oddest part, Gary says, is that very morning his fiancée had asked him what his guardian angel's name was – she'd had a dream about the angel. Coincidence? Not according to Gary and his friends. 'Everyone that's seen it agrees that it's an angel "swooping" down … I felt it go through me!'

Angelic Messengers

The word angel derives from the Greek angelos, which means messenger. In mythology, art, and religious texts, angels are frequently depicted as heavenly intermediaries who carry messages between the divine and the earthly realms.

The Bible frequently speaks of angels coming to earth to deliver important messages from God. According to the New Testament, an angel visited Mary to tell her she'd soon give birth to Jesus and when the baby was born, angels appeared to shepherds to announce the event. The Torah describes cherubim – the highest level of angels – as guarding the gates of Eden with flaming swords after Adam and Eve's banishment, to make sure God's will was carried out. In the Old Testament, angels give Moses the Ten Commandments, and Islam's holy book, the Qur'an, is said to have been presented to Mohammed by an angel named Jibreel.

In our everyday lives, angels continually perform their role as divine messengers, conveying information to us from the higher realms. These heavenly beings frequently communicate with us through thoughts and dreams, but also through visions and synchronicities (meaningful coincidences). The German philosopher, mystic, and theologian Meister Eckhart (c. 1260–1328), explained, 'That is all an angel is: an idea of God.'

Today, we seem every bit as eager as our ancestors to interact with angels. Peruse the Internet and you'll find hundreds of books, websites, blogs and other resources that claim to facilitate contact with your angels. You'll even see oracles (tools for divination) such as Kathy Tyler's popular *Angel Cards* and Doreen Virtue PhD's *Messages from Your Angels* card decks, which help you open your mind to receive angelic guidance.

The people who contributed pictures to this section believe angels chose to communicate with them, in many instances to provide comfort during difficult times. Some think departed loved ones shared messages of peace with them in order to ease their suffering. Others feel celestial entities brought them insights and information that helped them resolve challenging situations. Their fascinating photos support their stories and inspire us to look more deeply into the possibilities of inter-dimensional rapport.

An Angel Comforts a Grieving Woman

Michelle Brylowska of Epsom, Surrey, UK had recently lost two of the people who were nearest and dearest to her. Her father had passed away in June 2005 and then six months later her paternal grandmother had followed him to the Other Side. On 5 August 2006, as Brylowska stood at her grandmother Cahill's grave in County Cavan, Ireland, which is marked by a lovely Celtic cross headstone, a strange and beautiful light appeared. A radiant, rosy-red glow shimmered above the grave and within that light Brylowska saw an unusual, brilliant white image.

'A radiant, rosy-red glow shimmered above the grave ...'

With her mobile phone camera, she quickly snapped a picture of the winged being at the centre of the aurora borealis-like light. 'I am in no doubt that this is an angel!' she says.

The photo clearly shows a white figure with wings, apparently gazing down at Grandmother Cahill's grave. Did an angel really appear in order to comfort a grieving woman? That's what Brylowska believes. For her, the vision brought a message of peace and hope during a time of sadness and loss.

A Departed Father Visits his Family

Countless people report receiving communications from loved ones on the Other Side. Whether the contact occurs in the form of a vision, a dream, or something else, a message from a departed friend or relative gives hope to the bereaved that have been left behind.

For Janice Oppedal, the presence of a beautiful and inexplicable light shining in her garden brought a sense of overwhelming peace after the death in October 2009 of her beloved life partner Marty. Two months to the day after her eight-year-old son's father had passed, she took this picture. The brilliant light seemed otherworldly to her, and 'so bright it hurt to look at it!'

Oppedal explains, 'Marty always bought angel statues for me.' She believes the amazing light she saw that night was a bona fide angel, 'the real thing … a beautiful and true example of undying love!'

'The brilliant light seemed otherworldly to her …'

An Angelic Horseman

Like many other people who have lost loved ones, Crystal McDonald from Alberta, Canada, experienced what she believes was an inter-dimensional contact from the Other Side. Just four days after her father passed away suddenly from a heart attack, McDonald photographed this remarkable winged being flying above the hydrogen plant in Syncrude, Canada, where her father had worked for 29 years. 'To me it's quite an amazing looking picture,' she says. 'I believe [it] to be my dad.'

'Could this have been a hopeful sign of resurrection and rebirth?'

If you look closely at the photo McDonald snapped, you'll see it appears to show a rider astride a white, winged horse. Floating in a cloudless sky, the glowing white form is, indeed, amazing. According to Greek mythology, the fabled winged horse, Pegasus, sprang from drops of blood when Perseus cut off the head of the monster, Medusa. Could this unexpected sighting have been a hopeful sign conveyed to McDonald of resurrection and rebirth?

An Angel Brings Hope to a Murdered Boy's Family

One cool evening in 2007, a broken-hearted mother named Jodee Settle sat with her brother beside a campfire in her garden. Her 17-year-old son had recently been robbed and murdered, and Settle felt the boy's absence keenly. Instead of giving her comfort, the festive fire seemed to mock her sadness.

She expressed her feelings to her brother. 'I just lost my son and he [isn't] here anymore,' she said, and started walking away. Her brother, gazing into the fire, countered, 'Jodee, he is here.'

As she turned back, Settle saw a radiant orb hovering above the flames. It gave her a sense of encouragement in the midst her despair and she snapped a photo of it. 'Can you see the angel rising from the fire?' she asks.

'Settle saw a radiant orb hovering above the flames …'

Manhattan Firehouse Angel

Betty Jean Matthews' husband, a New York City firefighter, was one of the heroes lost during the 9/11 tragedy. A year after his death, Matthews attended the popular Macy's Thanksgiving Day Parade in Manhattan, along with the other firehouse families of Ladder 4, Engine 54, as she'd done with her husband when he was alive.

In this photo, Matthews stands beside the fire truck her husband knew so well. The brilliant white anomaly, she believes, is the spirit of her loved one joining her in this celebration. Sceptics might dismiss it as light reflecting off the shiny metal surface of the fire engine or perhaps camera lens flare. However, Matthews recalls: 'He said he would always be there for me. I think this picture proves that.'

'She believes the brilliant white anomaly is the spirit of her loved one ...'

Dad's Angel Visits his old High School

In 1980, 14-year-old Janine Davis of Pleasant Hill, California and her aunt travelled to Albuquerque, New Mexico to visit her father's side of the family. Janine's dad had died in a car accident when she was only two years old, and she missed him very much.

'Janine felt her father's presence and snapped a photo of the building ...'

During their trip, Janine's aunt took her to see Highland High School, where her father had been a student. Davis felt his presence there and she snapped a photo of the building with her Polaroid camera. When the picture developed, she saw the rainbow streaking in front of the school and thought to herself, 'How cool – this is my dad.'

She remembers, 'I heard a voice in my head saying, "I love you." I put [the photo] in my back pocket and knew that it was a message from him. I said, "I love you, too, Dad."'A copy of the photo has hung on her wall ever since.

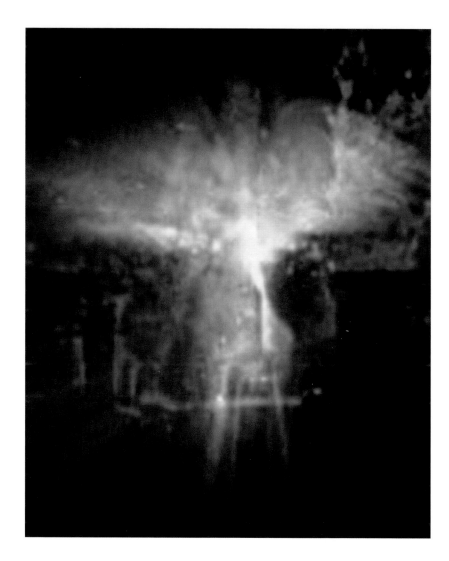

The Doidge Angel Caper

I n 2001, *The Sunday Times* announced the making of a Hollywood movie starring Marlon Brando, based on mysterious old film footage that reportedly featured an angel. According to the article, Danny Sullivan, author of *Ley Lines*, discovered the black-and-white film along with letters and other memorabilia in an antique shop in Monmouth, South Wales, and purchased the collection for £15. The letters told the story of William Doidge, a Monmouth-born soldier who fought in the Battle of Mons, Belgium, in 1914. Popular legend had it that during the battle, angels protected the British from defeat by the Germans.

'In 2002, BBC Wales exposed the clever publicity hoax ...'

Among the pile of correspondence, Sullivan found a letter written to Doidge in 1952 by an American GI identified only as 'Doug'. Doug related an angel war story of his own. One night, while his company trained on the grounds of Woodchester Park in the Cotswolds, an angel appeared to the soldiers – shortly before a bridge collapsed killing 20 men. Believing it might be the 'Mons Angel', Doidge began searching Woodchester nightly for the angel Doug had written about. Tucked in with the letters, Sullivan discovered a photograph of an angel floating above a cemetery. Had Doug or Doidge taken it?

After *The Sun* newspaper published the photo, musician John Reynolds contacted Sullivan to say he, too, had purchased some old film from the same antique store and that it depicted the same angel. Reynolds even used the picture on the cover of his album 'Interview With an Angel'. The story captured the imagination of the English media and the public until 2002, when BBC Wales exposed the clever publicity hoax. Sullivan, it turned out, had written a book about Woodchester Mansion's occult history and saw a chance to create a buzz around it. He and a friend in the PR business concocted the entire tale. William Doidge and the Woodchester angel never existed.

But what about the Angel of Mons? The legend may have evolved from Arthur Machen's novel, *The Bowmen and Other Legends of the War*, published a month after the Mons battle. Yet two weeks before publication of Machen's book, an English Brigadier-General named John Charteris described, in a letter to his wife, the appearance of angels turning back the Germans at Mons. We may never know the truth.

Angelic Visitors

What causes angels to visit earth? If F. Forrester Church, author of *Entertaining Angels*, is correct, angels actually reside among us all the time, even if we only notice them on rare occasions. Often, it seems, they show up to offer comfort, assist us in times of need, or bring messages from the divine realm. Many of the thousands of people who witnessed the appearance of the Lady of Light above St Mary's Coptic Church in Zeitoun, Egypt believed the Virgin Mary had come to give them her blessing. Sometimes angels appear to share information with us. Such was the case of Dr Frank Oski, a professor of pediatrics at John Hopkins University, whose story is told in Dr Melvin Morse's book *Parting Visions*. When the pediatrician was troubled by his inability to save the life of one of his young patients, an angel visited him and explained that life on earth was a 'cycle of improvements' in the development of human beings.

In other instances, such as in the photo taken in a church in Lavardin, France, angels may be drawn to holy sites and places where spiritual energy is concentrated. Some angel researchers suggest that something about the nature of water also attracts spirit beings. Tales abound of heavenly entities being sighted near bodies of water, among them St Bernadette's famous visions of the Madonna at Lourdes. Perhaps this is what occurred at the Wishing Well in County Cavan, Ireland?

The photos and stories in this section provide plenty of food for thought – and many fascinating angelic encounters captured on film by people around the world.

The Lady of Light Blesses St Mary's Coptic Church

On April 2, 1968, workmen in Zeitoun, Egypt (a district of Cairo) noticed a woman on the dome of St Mary's Coptic Church across the street. They feared she might jump to her death and called to her to be careful. Soon, pedestrians gathered to watch the woman. Christians in the crowd, however, insisted the figure on the dome wasn't human – it was the Virgin Mary visiting the church that had been named for her.

During the next few years, thousands of people – including scientists, religious authorities, and even Egypt's President Nasser – witnessed the appearance of the luminous figure. Often she moved about on the dome. Sometimes she bowed to the people in the street, seemingly blessing them. Numerous observers claimed to have undergone miraculous healings; many believed the Lady came to bring a message of peace. The visitations lasted for several minutes up to as long as two hours.

Canadian neuro-psychologist Michael Persinger and American geologist Dr John Derr proposed that seismic activity in the area could have caused what they called 'exotic luminous phenomena.' However, physicist Dr John Jackson, who analyzed the testimonies of eyewitnesses,

'Thousands of people witnessed the appearance of the luminous figure …'

recommended keeping an open mind. The sheer numbers who saw the apparition and the consistency of their reports suggested 'something very strange has happened here, perhaps something profound… that lies out of heretofore classical science.' A photo snapped by Wagih Rizk was confirmed as authentic by the Egyptian daily newspaper *El-Ahram* and published in 1968.

Wishing Well Angel

The couple on Rabbit Bridge at the Wishing Well in Kingscourt, County Cavan, Ireland, apparently have no idea that someone rather strange is standing nearby. But when Ben McKenna saw the photo he'd taken, he couldn't miss the figure of an ethereal-looking young woman only a dozen feet away from the pair.

What's odd about this picture? For one thing, the woman's feet are bare – an unlikely prospect on a chilly, damp, winter's day (the photo was taken in December 2008). Second, she's wearing a white, summery mini-dress that seems about 50 years out of date. Third, she's quite large in comparison to the men on the bridge.

Curious, McKenna checked to see if a statue had ever been positioned on the bridge; the answer was negative. Although, he says, the picture created quite a stir in the local Irish papers, the woman remains a mystery. Was an angel drawn to this enchanting spot?

'The woman's feet are bare – unlikely on a chilly, damp, winter's day ...'

Angel Sighted Through a Hunter's Lens

While hunting in Michigan, USA, David Ziegler got the surprise of a lifetime when his motion-sensor camera picked up activity in the area. The special hunting camera only takes photos when a moving object triggers its infrared sensor. This time, instead of snapping a deer or elk, the camera's lens captured an inexplicable, luminous being.

Ziegler took the incredible picture to a friend who owns a photography store to see what he thought of it. 'He said in over 25 years in business this was the coolest pic he ever saw. He couldn't debunk it.'

Is this a photo of an angel? The bluish-white figure appears to sport angel-like wings. Whatever it is, the entity displayed enough substance and movement to trip the camera's sensor – it wasn't simply light, mist or fog – and that's pretty amazing.

'Whatever it is, the entity displayed enough substance and movement to trip the camera's sensor ...'

An Angel Visits a Church in Lavardin

While visiting a church in Lavardin, near Vendôme, France, in September 1990, a tourist snapped this unusual apparition. Although hazy, the blue-white light has a vaguely human shape – but turn the picture upside-down and it clearly looks angelic, complete with wings and a crown-like halo. The photographer took numerous shots in the church that day, but only this one showed the strange luminous being, which rules out the possibility of defects in the camera or film.

Is this bright light the result of sun shining through a window and reflecting oddly on the camera's lens? Or is an angel standing on its head in the church sanctuary?

'turn the picture upside down and the blue-white shape clearly looks angelic ...'

An Apparition in a Hungarian Church

This amazing photograph shows what appears to be yet another spiritual being visiting a church. Art restorer Karoly Ligeti at the Karascond Church near Budapest, Hungary, claims that in September 1989 he witnessed the brilliant light from a scaffold in the church – although it remained unseen by other members of the congregation. Priest Béla Kovacs pointed out that no statue of this type existed in this location in the church at the time the photo was taken. He believes a genuine miracle occurred, and that the visiting entity was the Virgin Mary.

'He believes a genuine miracle occurred, and that the visiting entity was the Virgin Mary ...'

The photo is now displayed at the Karascond Church, where some parishioners say they see in it the Madonna holding the baby Jesus in her arms. Both the Hungarian Press Agency and Britain's Independent UFO Network examined the photo and found no evidence of doctoring. The picture was snapped before the advent of modern computer software such as Photoshop. Did a heavenly entity show up to participate in the church service? Or is there a more mundane explanation? The debate continues …

An Angel Attends a Christmas Pageant

While attending her church's Christmas pageant in December 2005, Casey Bowles of Desloge, Missouri, USA, took this photograph of the girls singing carols (at the left of the picture). When she viewed the photo later, however, she was surprised to see an unusual, bluish figure standing at the front of the church, near the piano player (at the far right of the picture) – a figure she hadn't noticed when she pressed the camera's shutter.

'You can see wings and a face,' Bowles points out. 'In some spots you can see through it [the angel].'

The luminous image does, indeed, resemble an angel with folded wings. We often envision angels singing in celestial choirs. Did this Missouri choir's heavenly music attract an angel to join the joyous Christmas pageant?

'When she viewed the photo, she was surprised to see an unusual, bluish figure ...'

An Angel Appears in Peterborough Cathedral

When Melvin Sutherland of Peterborough, UK, visited the city's beautiful gothic cathedral he wasn't expecting anything out of the ordinary to occur. Yet as he and a friend strolled through the sanctuary, Sutherland felt unexpected warmth near him, even though the vast, high-ceilinged space was rather chilly overall. Perplexed, he looked around, trying to determine the source of the peculiar warmth, but saw nothing to explain it.

'as he strolled through the sanctuary, Sutherland felt an unexpected warmth near him ...'

Pointing his digital camera in the direction of the warmth, Sutherland began snapping pictures, 'just for the fun of it,' he recalls. When he got home and downloaded the photos, however, he was in for quite a shock.

Angels, it seems, tend to gravitate toward churches, holy sites, and other places where spiritual energy is concentrated. Is the glowing white shape hovering before the cathedral's stained glass windows in Sutherland's photograph an angel? Did it generate the odd warmth he felt in the cold cathedral? Or was the anomaly produced by sunlight streaming through the windows or camera lens flare?

Christ Church's Cemetery Angel

Look closely and you'll see a small, winged creature hovering outside the stone walls of Christ Church in Linthwaite, West Yorkshire. Like many people who believe they've captured angels on film, Graham Jenkinson didn't notice the inexplicable form when he snapped this picture. But when he downloaded the photos he'd shot of the church, this strange bluish-white figure attracted his attention. Jenkinson says he was taking pictures of the church's graveyard – notice the headstone that appears at the bottom left of the frame.

Is the winged being an angel visiting the church? Or might it be the guardian of Sarah Ann, the person who's buried beneath this tombstone?

'Is the winged being an angel visiting the church?'

Two Angels Light Up a Florida Cemetery

From the time she was three years old, Donna Skoro's daughter had experienced things beyond the realm of what most people consider 'normal.' She often tried to tell her parents about the peculiarities she witnessed, but they discounted her tales as the products of a young girl's over-active imagination. 'We never really believed her until this photo, as well as others she took that year, proved us wrong,' admits her mother.

In 2001, now aged 27, she captured these beautiful lights – one gold and one blue – in a cemetery in Oviedo, Florida. Larger than a human being, they hovered above the graves, illuminating two headstones and a cross set between them.

'We believe the gold figure to the left could possibly be an angel,' Skoro says. 'If you look closely, you can definitely see the head, face and shoulders of the entity.' The blue-white light on the right, she thinks, might be two beings standing close together.

Are these angels visiting the graves of loved ones? The ghosts of the people buried there? Or a trick of light?

'Larger than a human being, they hovered above the graves ...'

Two Girls Encounter an Angel

One wintry night in 2007, 12-year-old Sheryl was staying with her family and a 15-year-old friend at a cabin in Winthrop near Seattle, Washington. Sheryl had just received a new digital camera as a Christmas gift and the girls decided to practise taking photos with it. As they began snapping photos outdoors, they spotted a strange, glowing image on the camera's LCD screen. Sensing an eerie silence around them, they nervously hurried back into the cabin.

When they downloaded the pictures to the computer, they noticed this strange, misty shape against the starry background. The wispy figure appears to be a woman wearing long, flowing robes and raising one hand, perhaps to greet them or confer a blessing. The apparition may be holding a baby and her hair and robe show surprising detail.

Is the figure an angel or spirit manifesting to the girls? Or was the anomaly caused by moisture or fog, or perhaps the photographer's breath, in the chilly, damp air?

'Sensing an eerie silence around them, they nervously hurried back into the cabin ...'

Grandmother's Angel Visits at Christmas

On Christmas Eve 1999, Brad and his family gathered at his mother's house in Malvern, Ohio, to celebrate the holiday. For as long as he could remember, his grandmother had been present for the festivities. She'd lived with them for many years and helped raise Brad and his four brothers, but she'd passed away earlier that year. This was the first Christmas his grandmother wasn't with them. And yet, she was.

As his brother strung lights on their evergreen tree outdoors, Brad's daughter snapped a photo with his new digital camera. The luminous silhouette that appeared in front of the tree looks just like an angel: 'Our grandmother's angel,' Brad believes.

'This was the first Christmas his grandmother wasn't with them ...'

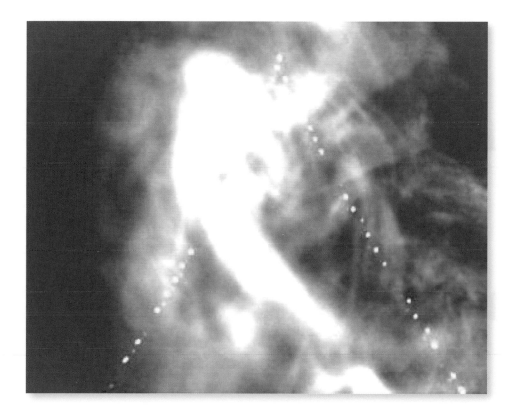

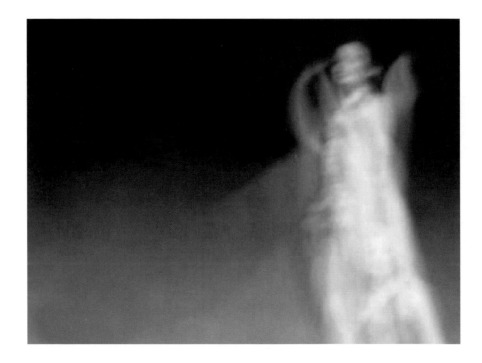

A Dancing Angel

In 2007, Fabio and his wife attended their daughter's dance recital. As they sat in the audience at the school's auditorium, the proud mother snapped photos of her daughter and the other young dancers. Among the pictures she took was one they couldn't explain.

'This beautiful image of an angel was on our digital camera, but not on stage!' Fabio says. He recalls they took the camera to a photographer, 'who said he never saw an image like this in 30 years. He was amazed.' The unexplained photograph made a huge impression on Fabio and his family. '[It] changed our lives,' he says, and led him to begin researching angels.

The radiant figure depicted in this picture is so vivid and colourful, she looks practically human. Could a dancer have appeared momentarily on stage, and then exited, before the photographer realized she'd captured the image with her camera? Using a slow shutter speed in low lighting could have caused a blurred image such as this one. Or did an angel really join the young dancers in their recital?

'This beautiful image of an angel was on our digital camera, but not on stage ...'

A Mysterious Angel Shadows an Anonymous Couple

This intriguing photo remains a mystery, despite the fact that it's circulated on the Internet for many years. Behind the unidentified couple we can clearly see a full-body form that resembles an angel wearing a long white gown. However, the man and woman in the foreground of the picture seem completely unaware of the entity's presence. Is it guarding them? Bringing them a message?

'the man and woman in the foreground seem completely unaware of the entity's presence ...'

Based on the couple's hairstyles and countenances, the black and white photo seems to have been taken several decades ago, yet the date and place it records are unknown. Most likely this picture predates sophisticated computer technology, however, and thus the ethereal image in the background probably wasn't added into the composition by computer manipulation. But what exactly are we viewing? Is it a paranormal occurrence, or does the extraordinary effect have a much more ordinary explanation?

Angelic Interventions

Angels often appear at the moment when we most need their help. In the biblical story of Daniel in the lion's den, an angel intervened to save his life. Another story from the book of Daniel tells of three Jewish men named Shadrach, Meshach and Abednego whom an angel rescued from death in a fiery furnace. In the 18th century, the Englishman William Cowper, poet and composer of many popular hymns, had decided to end his life. He hired a hackney driver to take him to the River Thames, where he planned to drown himself. A thick fog soon engulfed them, however, and they lost their way. After driving around for some time, they found themselves right back at Cowper's home. He felt an angel had drawn him into the fog and saved his life.

Today, angels still show up just in the nick of time. According to a Gallup Poll conducted in 2007, three-quarters of Americans believe in angels, and many say their lives have been directly affected by divine intervention. James Redfield, author of the best-selling book *The Celestine Prophecy*, believes angels intervened on his behalf on several occasions. Once he fell 40 feet onto concrete, without being injured. Another time he crashed through a ceiling in a shopping mall and landed on a glass display case, but didn't even get a scratch. Both times, Redfield says, an entity wrapped him in an invisible bubble that protected him from harm.

The people whose stories appear in this section are convinced of the presence of angels and their miraculous powers to heal and protect us. Not only did these individuals live to tell of their amazing experiences, they even took photos of their celestial guardians.

A Hospital Angel Brings a Miraculous Healing

On 5 November 2008, as millions of Americans prepared for the holiday season, Chelsea Banton lay in Presbyterian Hemby Children's Hospital in Charlotte, North Carolina, waiting to die. The 14-year-old girl, who had struggled her entire life with debilitating birth defects, had been taken off life support and seemed ready to succumb to pneumonia after spending seven weeks in the hospital. While her family prepared to say goodbye, the hospital's security monitor registered an unusual bright light glowing in the hall outside Chelsea's room.

Several hospital workers also noticed the brilliant light, which resembled a winged form about the size of a human being. They pointed it out to Chelsea's mother, Colleen, who immediately responded, 'Oh, wow, that's an angel!'

She believed the angel had come either to heal Chelsea or to take the girl to heaven, and quickly snapped a picture of the strange, beautiful light with her mobile phone camera.

'Several hospital workers also noticed the brilliant light, which resembled a winged form ...'

Within an hour, Chelsea started to improve. Three days later, she was able to go home and celebrated her 15th birthday with her family on Christmas Day. Colleen is convinced an angel intervened and saved her daughter's life. 'It's a blessing. It's a miracle,' Banton told NBC's *The Today Show*.

Driver had an Angel Looking Over her Shoulder

In November 1998, as Rose Benvenuto of Pawling, New York, drove home late in the evening, a dog dashed in front of her car. Benvenuto swerved to avoid hitting it, smashing the car in the process. Despite the mangled state of the vehicle, Benvenuto received only a minor arm injury in the accident.

'Despite the mangled state of her vehicle, Benvenuto received only a minor arm injury ...'

This photograph, taken shortly after the accident by Sharon Boo, photographer with the Pawling Fire Department, may reveal why Benvenuto escaped serious injury or even death. The mysterious, luminous figure standing beside the wreck looks like an angel – it even appears to have wings. Could this be the driver's guardian angel, who protected her during the crash? Boo certainly thinks so. Having viewed the accident scene and the photo she snapped, she believes Benvenuto 'had an angel looking over her shoulder.'

An Angel Heals a Teenager in Michigan

Scott Monroe's son was scheduled for surgery the day after he snapped this photo of the Michigan teenager and his girlfriend in 2007. Doctors had discovered ominous-looking lumps in the boy's stomach and advised Monroe to prepare himself for the worst. At the time this photo was taken, the girl's grandfather, a retired pastor, was holding a prayer meeting for Monroe's son. Is the brilliant white figure his guardian angel, ready to accompany him into surgery?

The next day, during the operation, the boy's doctors discovered the lumps in his stomach had diminished in size and weren't harmful. 'They did not know why,' Monroe recalls. In fact, the lumps appeared to be going away. Remarkably, within a week the lumps had completely disappeared.

Larry Dossey MD's book *Prayer is Good Medicine*, provides strong evidence that prayer works miracles. According to Dr Todd Michael, an emergency room physician and author of *The Evolution Angel*, angels 'enable your prayers to be carried out by becoming those prayers.' Is that what occurred in this instance? Did the prayer groups' thoughts produce the angel in this photograph to heal the teenager?

'Doctors had discovered ominous-looking lumps in the boy's stomach ...'

Spirit Beings

Spirit beings are often thought to be non-physical guides or guardians, angels or ancestors who've crossed over to the Other Side. The spiritual teachings, mythologies, and folklore of cultures around the world describe numerous entities that exist in our world as well as the one beyond. Irish legends often include fairies and leprechauns. The indigenous peoples of North America recognize spirits in all aspects of nature and believe spirit animals or totems watch over them here on earth. Esoteric writings describe beings called sylphs, salamanders, gnomes, and undines who serve as ambassadors from the four elemental realms. Hindu mythology speaks of devas, benevolent supernatural beings who guide nature's progress.

Psychics and other sensitive individuals say they can see these spirits. They also view haloes, luminous forms, and bright, whitish streaks of ectoplasm (a vaporous substance from which spirits and ghosts are supposedly formed) emanating from human beings. What these psychics may be observing is commonly called an 'aura', the subtle and usually invisible energy field that surrounds the body. The photo 'Angel or Aura?' may depict this vital energy.

Aura imaging cameras claim to be able to photograph the human aura. The person being photographed holds a sensor connected to a Polaroid camera. The sensor registers the resonance of the subject's electromagnetic field and delivers it to the camera, which records the coloured lights that are usually invisible around the head and shoulders. However, the method's accuracy has

been disputed because the colours in Polaroid prints change depending on the speed of development.

Occasionally, ordinary cameras also capture what might be a spirit or an aura. The photos in this section present an array of intriguing possibilities and make us wonder: are we alone, or do unseen beings accompany us on our earthly journey?

Spirit Beings Gather on Mount Shasta

During August 2004, Karl Barrett and a group of friends visited Mount Shasta, California, the second highest volcano in the US, soaring more than 14,000 feet above sea level. A prominent landmark on an ancient Native American trade route, it falls midway between San Francisco and Portland, Oregon. The group was on a spiritual retreat. When Eric Peterson snapped this photograph they were calling on the 'Great Presence of Light' to join them in the same spot where St Germaine first appeared to Godfré Ray King (aka Guy Ballard), founder of the I AM Activities and author of *Unveiled Mysteries*.

'There were many very high beings present at the time,' Barrett recalls, and he isn't referring to the altitude. Claire Heartsong, author of the book *Anna, Grandmother of Jesus*, was sitting just outside the photographer's range, preparing to channel the entity known as 'Anna.' The dramatic streaks of light spotlighting Barrett's companions – and also perhaps emanating from them – suggest that powerful energies were flowing between the group and the higher realms at the time this photo was taken. As Barrett explains, 'The photo reveals another dimensional reality, which is part of us and we are part of it.'

Are these baffling light displays caused by camera glitches or environmental factors? Or are we seeing the amazing portraits of divine beings?

'The dramatic streaks of light spotlighting Barrett's companions suggest that powerful energies were flowing between the group and the higher realms ...'

Spirit Beings on Australia's Gold Coast

On 18 July 2003, after a day of shopping in Harbour Town in Brisbane, Queensland, Lana and her friend stopped around 6.30pm to buy seafood at a waterfront shop on Australia's Gold Coast. The women had just ordered their fish and calamari dinners and taken them down to the sandy beach to eat. They snapped some pictures with Lana's digital camera using a night setting, self-timer and flash. Lana says she didn't notice she'd only set the camera's resolution to e-mail size, so the quality of the photos is rather poor and grainy.

As she prepared to take the pictures, Lana recalls, 'I could see something strange on my viewer … I definitely noticed the winged one on the screen and the wavy energy from the other two.' Indeed, one of the photos shows what appear to be beautiful, glowing, orange wings. Is it an angel, or another type of spirit being? A friend who saw the photos suggested they might reveal Lana's spirit animal guide or totem – if you look closely, you can see what resemble the eyes of a cat or eagle.

Altogether, Lana took 14 photos that depict the strange auroras. Although she says she's always felt a close connection to her spirit guides, she didn't expect them to show up in brilliant colour that evening and to allow themselves to be photographed. She notes, however, that the ocean right behind the women as they stood on the beach could have been a conductor for the spirit energy.

Sceptics might explain the peculiar lights in these photos as camera-related anomalies. Orange, hazy glows can be caused by extended exposure settings and flash delays on digital cameras when taking pictures at night. But it's also possible spirit beings decided to join in the women's holiday fun.

'if you look closely, you can see what resemble the eyes of a cat or eagle …'

Avebury's Glowing Orbs

In such a mystical place as the stone circle at Avebury, not far from Stonehenge, perhaps it's no surprise to see unusual and perhaps supernatural lights in the sky. These glowing orbs floating above the stones have been photographed numerous times.

Of course, the orbs in the photos could be anomalies caused by a digital camera's flash reflecting off moisture or dust mites in the air, which can produce such effects.

However, the unexplained orbs have also been seen by the naked eye. Are the orbs otherworldly spirits drawn to this ancient and magical site, where almost anything seems possible, or merely tricks of light?

'Are the orbs otherworldly spirits drawn to this ancient and magical site?'

A Healer's Spiritual Energy

Charlotte Evans of Española, New Mexico believes, 'The power of spirit or energy is within all of us.' Evans feels this photograph may portray that powerful energy emanating from her mother, Apostle Elizabeth Hairston. Hairston ministers in churches around the world, and according to Evans, she also possesses the gift of healing.

'Does this picture show the force of Hairston's magnetic spiritual energy flowing around her?'

During her services, Hairston often wears a glittering blue cape embellished with 10,000 beads. In this photo, her feet seem to be levitating slightly off the floor. Does this picture show the force of Hairston's magnetic spiritual energy flowing around her? Are the rays of bright light ectoplasm? Or is this an example of what can transpire when a photographer takes a picture using a digital camera with an extended shutter speed in artificial light? The orange glow and streaks are characteristic of this type of anomaly, generated by movement in this kind of situation. It's also possible that the shiny beads on the blue cape might reflect light in an unusual way. Hairston may indeed embody great spiritual power, but it's uncertain whether this photo actually captures anything supernatural.

Two Girls' Spirits Appear at Their Graves

In August 2006, on the anniversary of her two nieces' deaths, Debra Boyett of Paris, Texas, visited their graves and took this photo showing amorphous blue lights and orbs that may be ectoplasm. The sisters, aged eight and 12, had died the previous year in a house fire.

What caused the strange, hazy light effects shown here? The time of year rules out the possibility of smoke or mist that often appears during cold weather. Does the unusual glow indicate the presence of the girls' spirits, coming to comfort their bereaved aunt?

'The sisters, aged eight and 12, had died the previous year in a house fire ...'

A Girl's Spirit Brings Solace in the Sunset

On a beautiful summer night in 2006, Janis Ohm and her friend watched the setting sun. The day before, her friend had buried her 15-year-old daughter, Tara, who had died in an accident. As the women sought solace in the peaceful scene, Ohm snapped photos of the sunset. Later, when she viewed the pictures, she was surprised to find bright white orbs and glowing clouds of what may be ectoplasm. 'I have taken a lot of pictures before but have never seen angels and orbs like that night,' Ohm explains. Are these mysterious lights evidence of Tara's spirit comforting her grieving mother? Or did the anomalies result from vaporous mist in the atmosphere?

'The day before, her friend had buried her 15-year-old daughter, Tara, who had died in an accident ...'

Angel or Aura?

It's difficult to determine what this unusual photograph that Monique took of her sister actually shows. The bright, blue-white lights appear to overlay the girl's body and flare out from her on either side. Monique admits she's perplexed, too, and says, 'I'm not sure if it is a ghost or an angel, but after I had a close look at the photo, it shows a woman with glasses and wings.'

The flash settings on digital cameras can create strange light effects, as other photographs in this book reveal. The blue colour and the positions of the lights in this image, however, are different than the hazy, orangey glows and white streaks that typically occur. Monique's photo more closely resembles those taken with aura imaging cameras, which are used to photograph the human aura or energy field surrounding a person's body. Does this picture show her sister's aura? The presence of a spirit? Or something else entirely?

'The bright, blue-white lights appear to overlay the girl's body and flare out from her on either side ...'

Angels in Clouds, Water and Smoke

Looking for signs and omens in clouds, water and smoke is an ancient practice. Early seafarers observed patterns in the sky and sea to help them navigate the globe. Three millennia ago, astrologers at the imperial Chinese court studied not only the stars, but also clouds and rain to divine the future. The native peoples of North and South America have long sought guidance from nature. Even today, we look to the heavens for signs and messages. When a deep red sun sets on the horizon we know the next day will be hot. A hazy ring around the moon indicates rain is coming soon. And, of course, a rainbow is a universal sign of hope and good luck.

So perhaps it's no surprise that many people see angels in clouds, water and even smoke. The shifting shapes trigger imagination and intuition. 'The intuitive sense allows us to go beyond the normal mind,' writes Sarvananda Bluestone PhD in *How to Read Signs and Omens in Everyday Life*. 'It is our doorway to new sight – to new vision … Each of us has the power, privilege, and the right to see the divine in a candle or a burning bush.'

The rejuvenating energy in water may attract angels and other spirits. Mythology, folklore, and religious texts frequently describe sightings of otherworldly entities near bodies of water, one of the best known being St Teresa's visions of the Madonna at Lourdes, France. The Arthurian Legends speak of the Lady of the Lake, a supernatural character possessing great wisdom and power. Holy sites and healing spas are often established at springs, lakes or the seaside – perhaps angels and deities drawn to these spots provide the uplifting vibrations visitors experience.

Smoke, too, may possess mystical properties. Buddhists invoke the spirit of the Buddha by burning incense. The rising smoke is said to carry prayers to the deities. Both Catholics and pagans cleanse their sacred spaces with incense smoke. Some psychics gaze into smoke to induce a light trance, in order to see visions of the future. Perhaps the photographs in this section enable us and the people who took them also to see beyond the veil.

An Angel Appears in the Dollywood Fountain

Angelia Reedy had enjoyed a pleasurable outing with her daughter and stepdaughter at Dollywood – country singer Dolly Parton's family amusement park at Pigeon Forge in the Great Smoky Mountains, eastern Tennessee. As the two girls sat beside a fountain at the park, Reedy snapped their picture to commemorate the visit in 2005.

When she received the photos back from the lab, the results surprised her, to say the least. 'The picture of the girls had this angel in the water.' According to Reedy, 'When taking the picture of them, I did not see an angel; when I viewed the pictures on my digital camera, there were no angels in the background.'

Baffled, Reedy phoned Dollywood to see if they intentionally shaped the water in the fountain to form images. The staff assured her they did not. The second photo shows the fountain as it normally appears.

'Angel researchers say that angels are attracted by laughter and joy, as well as by water …'

Angel researchers say that angels are attracted by laughter and joy, as well as by water. Did an angel turn up to share in the Reedy family's fun that day? After all, the photographer's name is Angelia!

A Fountain Attracts the Madonna and Child

Here's another amazing photo of an apparition in a fountain, this one shot at Center Parcs Holiday Village, Norfolk, UK. This unexplained image, taken in 1995, bears a striking resemblance to a woman with an infant in her arms. The shining white-gold light and what look like radiant, transparent robes immediately make us think of Mary holding the baby Jesus.

The life-giving energy inherent in moving water, which Austrian scientist Wilhelm Reich called 'orgone', is believed by many to attract spirits. That's why a number of photos in this book, and others you'll see online, depict angelic shapes around bodies of water. Of course, nearby light sources or the camera's flash reflecting off the water might have produced this glowing shape when the camera's shutter froze the sparkling, falling water in time. Perhaps our preconceptions cause us to interpret it as the Madonna and Child.

Does this photo represent another trick of the eye; a religious concept projected onto an ordinary, worldly environment? Or are we actually witnessing the appearance of a divine entity?

'This unexplained image bears a striking resemblance to a woman with an infant in her arms ...'

A Fisherman's Angel

Bill Ehman of Charleston, West Virginia, USA had been in deep prayer for a few days when a friend invited him to go fishing on 21 October 1997. The weather was cold, cloudy, and windy – hardly

'Ehman believes the angel in the photo came to him in response to his prayers ...'

ideal fishing weather – as they cast their lines into Summit Lake. But around 2.30pm, Ehman caught a trout – and surprisingly the wind calmed and the temperature rose until it seemed more like spring than late fall. The sun came out and as Ehman watched it reflect off the water, he snapped this brilliant photo. However, what he photographed was, he says, 'nothing like what you see in this picture. I saw no image above the water.'

Ehman believes the angel in the photo came to him in response to his prayers. It gave him hope. He now shares the picture with people in nursing homes who, like him, seek answers to their prayers.

A Celestial Conundrum

During a storm in Hinesville, Georgia, USA a newspaper photographer took this intriguing picture while trying to shoot lightning. However, he wasn't the only person to capture this angel on film that day in 1996. Shelley was recuperating in Georgia after a long illness when she snapped this photo – although she didn't notice the angel until after the prints came back from the lab. She says: 'I have since kept it in a frame, next to my bed, believing it protected me from becoming ill, again . . . which surprisingly, I haven't.'

Then in 2005, after www.angelsghosts.com posted the photos on its site, Adam, from San Antonio, Texas, reported having a picture of the angel, too. According to him, the image, which he'd been carrying in his wallet for about ten years, was taken from an aeroplane window by a friend of his aunt. Soon after, Sharon from Billerica, Massachusetts, sent in yet another photo of the angel, which she said a friend shot in Florida. Next to weigh-in was Lori, whose relative supposedly snapped the picture at her great aunt's funeral in Lincoln, Nebraska, in January 1996.

The photo continued to generate interest and confusion, as more and more people submitted copies – each with a different story. A man claimed the picture was taken in 1994 at a Mendenhall, Mississippi cemetery during the burial of John L. Sullivan. Matt from Toronto, Canada, got his copy from a man his aunt knew. Denise's aunt gave her the angel photo, which she believes was taken during the Oklahoma bombing in 1995.

'The photo continued to generate interest and confusion, as more and more people submitted copies – each with a different story ...'

When and where did this photo really originate? Who actually took it, and how did it fall into the hands of so many unrelated people? The mystery may never be solved. Denise's comment provides inspirational food for thought: 'I think if anything it is a message that we are never alone.'

Angels Leave a Burning House

As his mother-in-law's lovely old house burned in July 2002, Jay snapped this incredible photo. Plainly visible on the roof of the porch are what appear to be figures, exiting the house as smoke billows around them. 'I see two distinct angels: one a man, the other a woman with a baby in her arms,' says Jay.

The larger-than-life figures, with their wings and white robes, do look remarkably like angels. Are they the family's guardians, come to protect them from the fire? The ghosts of previous occupants? Or merely a mirage in the smoke?

'Plainly visible on the roof of the porch are what appear to be figures, exiting the house as smoke billows around them ...'

A Heavenly Heart Offers Guidance and Hope

After fisherman and writer Mark Williams, from Gloucester, Massachusetts, died unexpectedly of a heart attack, his personal and creative partner, fellow writer Kathleen Valentine, felt terribly bereft. Even though he'd departed this earth physically, she wanted to keep his memory alive by republishing a book he'd written. The original edition had gone out of print, but Valentine collaborated with Williams' mother and photographer Jay Albert to bring out a revised, memorial edition packed with photos.

However, Williams' mother insisted on deleting some parts of the book that reflected unfavourably on the family. Torn between her desire to see Williams' book back in print and her wish to remain true to the deceased author's story and vision, Valentine debated about how to proceed. She discussed her concerns with Albert, who urged her to go forward with the project. Finally, in July 2008 she agreed to make the book available again to Williams' readers, albeit in revised form.

The day she sent the new edition of the book to the printer, Albert shot this photo of a cloud shaped like a heart. Says Valentine: 'We both saw it as Mark's approval.'

'Even though he'd departed this earth physically, she wanted to keep his memory alive ...'

Angel in a Starry Sky

At first glance this image appears to be an abstract splash of fire and ice. But look closely and you'll see the face and torso of a beautiful female angel, her majestic wings spread wide against a starry sky. Zoom in and you'll notice details, such as her elaborate, jewelled crown.

'look closely and you'll see the face and torso of a beautiful female angel, her majestic wings spread wide against a starry sky ...'

According to Christy Stover, the picture was taken in Montrose, Colorado in 1996 for a photography contest of stars at night – although the photographer didn't realize she'd captured an angel on film until she picked up the finished prints. The man who developed the photos, however, spotted the angel right away.

'Some people can see it,' Stover says, whereas others 'have stared at it for hours and still can't.' Stover thinks, 'This was captured for a reason so people will believe.'

Ocean Spray Angel

Three months after her husband's death, Flora Walker watched the waves crashing on the rocks at Shore Acres Park in Coos Bay, Oregon. As she snapped photos of the ocean, she recalls: 'I was talking to God, telling him how much I missed my husband and how I wished he was there with me.'

Later, when she viewed the pictures she'd taken, she saw the angel emerging from the surf. 'I knew Jim was letting me know he made it to heaven,' she explains. When her husband became ill, she'd given him a statue of an angel, which he loved. 'This angel is in the same stance as the one I gave him.'

'I knew Jim was letting me know he made it to heaven …'

Xcaret Angel

Considered by many to be a magical place, Xcaret, located on Mexico's Yucatan Peninsula, was once completely hidden under the sea. When a meteor crashed to earth millions of years ago, the area emerged from the subterranean world. Today, tourists come to visit the underground rivers and caves that lie beneath Xcaret's surface and to see the thousands of holes called cenonotes that dapple the land. The ancient Maya considered these holes sacred and believed they led to Xibalba, the Mayan underworld.

Ron and Linda Martinez were on holiday in this mystical spot when they shot this beautiful photograph using a 35mm underwater camera.

The white robed and winged being floating above a placid, green pool certainly looks angelic. Its head, torso and hand are remarkably clear and it seems pleasantly at home in the serene environment. After witnessing this vision, the couple said, 'Our intention is to share this photograph with the world.'

'The white robed and winged being floating above a placid, green pool certainly looks angelic ...'

A Mother's Angel Accompanies her Daughter

One month before Joyce Drudge of Toronto, Canada, snapped this photograph in July 2008, her mother died of cancer. She'd wanted to die at her home in Labrador, Quebec, so Joyce had stayed with her until the end. Before she passed, Joyce's mother told her, 'When you go back to Toronto, I'm going with you.'

'Joyce felt she was seeing her mother and grandmother, safe in heaven ...'

As Joyce and a friend drove back to Toronto, she glanced up at the sky. 'The sun was going down and this one cloud was lit up,' she recalls. Quickly, she snapped a picture with her mobile phone camera.

In the cloud, Joyce saw three figures. To her, the one in the centre looked like Jesus, holding another being in each of his arms. Joyce felt she was seeing her mother and grandmother, safe in heaven. 'She came back to Toronto with me as an angel,' Joyce says.

New Bedford Angel

New Bedford, Massachusetts, USA is better known for its fishing industry (and formerly for whaling) than for angel sightings. But when Mike Valeri, photographer for *The Standard-Times* of New Bedford, published this photograph of a cloudy sunset over Padanaram Harbor in nearby South Dartmouth, the paper received an enthusiastic response from readers.

Many people pointed out the angel hovering in the clouds, at the top right of the photo – something Valeri hadn't noticed when he pressed the shutter or even after his picture appeared in print. When the paper ran the photo again, readers began requesting copies – so many that the newspaper decided to sell the prints and donate the proceeds to needy families at Christmas.

'Many people pointed out the angel hovering in the clouds, at the top right of the photo – something Valeri hadn't noticed ...'

The Lady in the Falls

According to Indian legend, during a time of great suffering and death among the tribes who lived near Niagara Falls, the people sought to appease the Thunder God, Hinum, by sending a beautiful maiden over the Falls in a canoe laden with

'the people sought to appease the Thunder God, Hinum, by sending a beautiful maiden over the Falls in a canoe laden with offerings ...'

offerings. When it came time for the chief's daughter to be sacrificed, she made an agreement with Hinum's sons. She would remain forever in the Falls if they would reveal the secret behind the tribe's woes and allow her to share it with her people so they might survive.

In 1988, Dawn Campbell photographed what she believes to be the mythological Lady in the Falls (also known as the Maid of the Mist). These photos show the Falls as well as what appears to be a close up of a woman's face. Campbell describes her reaction when she saw the picture: 'It astounded me! I have heard so many stories about the Lady in the Falls, and I do wonder if perhaps I captured her ...'

An Angel Flies Over New Mexico

This striking cloud formation certainly resembles an angel with its wings spread wide as it flies through the sky. Janice Garcia of Las Cruces, New Mexico took the picture with her mobile phone camera. Garcia was driving back to work after her lunch break when the angel appeared overhead. Although the figure's head, body and wings are quite distinct, Garcia says it was much clearer when she first spotted it. However, by the time she pulled over to the side of the road and managed to snap the photo, the cloud's shape had softened and dissipated somewhat. Still, it's a beautiful and inspiring shot.

'Garcia was driving back to work after her lunch break when the angel appeared overhead ...'

An Angel in a Stormy Sky

Many people recount stories of angels appearing to them during challenging times in their lives. Cynthia Dickerson is one of them. These individuals often say the presence of spiritual guardians provided inspiration, solace, or guidance when it was needed most.

When Dickerson took this dramatic picture in May 2007, she recalls: 'I needed a spiritual boost in my life.' She'd taken her new camera out into an empty field near her home in western Tennessee and begun snapping photos of the pending storm. There amidst the dark clouds she spotted a bright symbol of hope – an angelic light shining though the stormy sky. Dickerson, who has always believed in angels, 'found comfort in knowing I was the one who saw it.'

'the presence of spiritual guardians provided inspiration, solace, or guidance when it was needed most ...'

A Sign from Above

Michael believes the angel in the picture he took during the summer of 2007 was a sign from above. He'd just finished speaking on the phone with a friend about the difficult time he was going through. As he stood alone in his back yard, thinking, 'Give me a sign, please,' he gazed up at the reddish clouds in the sky. Suddenly, the clouds dispersed – all except the figure shown in his photograph. The angel hovered above him for about ten minutes, he recalls, then quickly disappeared. It was the sign Michael had requested. 'I had such a feeling of calm,' he says.

'Later in the day, when he drove home, the picture was gone …'

As if that was not enough, Michael received another sign the following day. While sitting in traffic, he glanced out of his car window and noticed a picture posted only a foot or so away. It resembled the cloud angel he'd seen from his back yard the day before. On it he read the words: 'Someone up there likes you!' Later in the day, when he drove home, the picture was gone. 'In the following days I made some life-changing decisions,' he remembers, 'and life has been great ever since.'

Acknowledgments

I wish to thank all the people who contributed their inspiring photographs and stories to this book. Thanks, too, to Sarah Callard, Neil Baber, and Paula Munier of F+W Publications for making this book possible, and to Louis Charles who operates the www.angelsghosts.com website for providing photos and assistance.

About the Author

Skye Alexander is the author of more than 30 fiction and non-fiction books. Her stories have appeared in numerous anthologies internationally, and her work has been translated into more than a dozen languages. She was featured in the Discovery Channel TV special *Secret Stonehenge*. After spending thirty-one years in Massachusetts, she now lives in Texas.

Picture Credits

These images have come from many sources and acknowledgment has been made wherever possible. If images have been used without due credit or acknowledgment, through no fault of our own, apologies are offered. If notified, the publisher will be pleased to rectify any errors or omissions in future editions.

Index